HENRY HUDSON AND THE MURDEROUS ARCTIC MUTINY

by John Micklos, Jr. • illustrated by Martín Bustamante

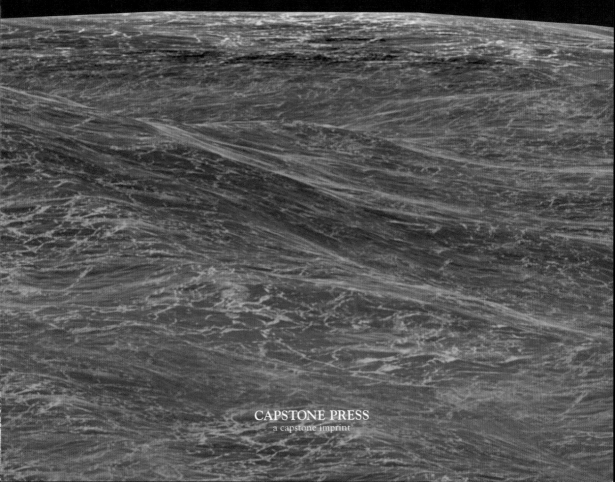

CAPSTONE PRESS
a capstone imprint

Published by Capstone Press, an imprint of Capstone
1710 Roe Crest Drive, North Mankato, Minnesota 56003
capstonepub.com

Library of Congress Cataloging-in-Publication Data is available on the Library of
Congress website.

ISBN: 9781666390544 (hardcover)
ISBN: 9781666390490 (paperback)
ISBN: 9781666390506 (ebook PDF)

Summary: In 1610, English explorer Henry Hudson set sail in search of the fabled
Northwest Passage. But when icy waters stranded Hudson and the *Discovery* in a
bay for the winter, tensions flared. The crew lost faith in their captain and began
to plot . . . mutiny!

Editorial Credits
Editor: Abby Huff; Designer: Dina Her; Production Specialist: Tori Abraham

All internet sites appearing in back matter were available and accurate when this
book was sent to press.

Printed and bound in the USA. 809195

TABLE OF CONTENTS

In April 1610, the *Discovery* sat in London Harbor, England. Soon, its crew would begin a daring voyage. They would sail roughly 3,000 miles across the Atlantic Ocean. From there, they would seek the Northwest Passage. Explorers believed this water route ran through the Arctic to Asia. Was the passage real or a myth? No one knew.

If we find this new route to Asia, we will become famous.

Discovery's crew included 23 men. The captain was famed navigator Henry Hudson. His son John was among the crew.

Also aboard was mate Robert Juet, who had sailed with Hudson before. Juet was a skilled sailor, but he had a bad temper.

Crew member Abacuk Pricket kept a journal throughout the journey.

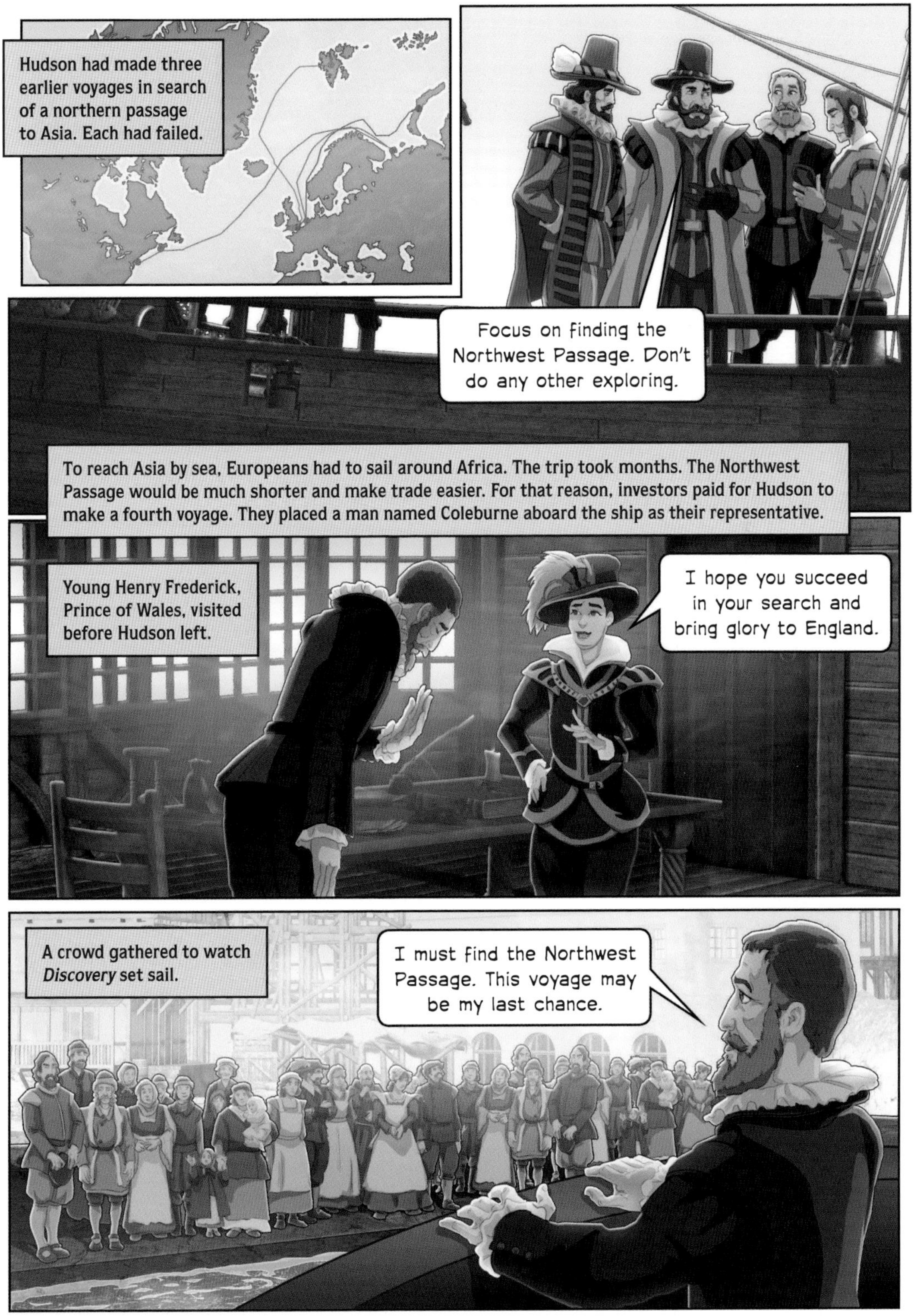
Hudson had made three earlier voyages in search of a northern passage to Asia. Each had failed.
Focus on finding the Northwest Passage. Don't do any other exploring.
To reach Asia by sea, Europeans had to sail around Africa. The trip took months. The Northwest Passage would be much shorter and make trade easier. For that reason, investors paid for Hudson to make a fourth voyage. They placed a man named Coleburne aboard the ship as their representative.
Young Henry Frederick, Prince of Wales, visited before Hudson left.
I hope you succeed in your search and bring glory to England.
A crowd gathered to watch *Discovery* set sail.
I must find the Northwest Passage. This voyage may be my last chance.

Discovery sailed down the River Thames. The trip got off to a rough start. Hudson argued with Coleburne, the investors' representative, before the ship even reached open sea. Hudson sent him back to London.

The next part of the journey went more smoothly. *Discovery* reached Iceland in mid-May. The crew stopped and explored. They hunted and fished. They bathed in hot springs.

While on shore in Iceland, Henry Greene got into a fistfight with the ship's doctor. Hudson and Greene were friends. The captain took Greene's side in the argument.

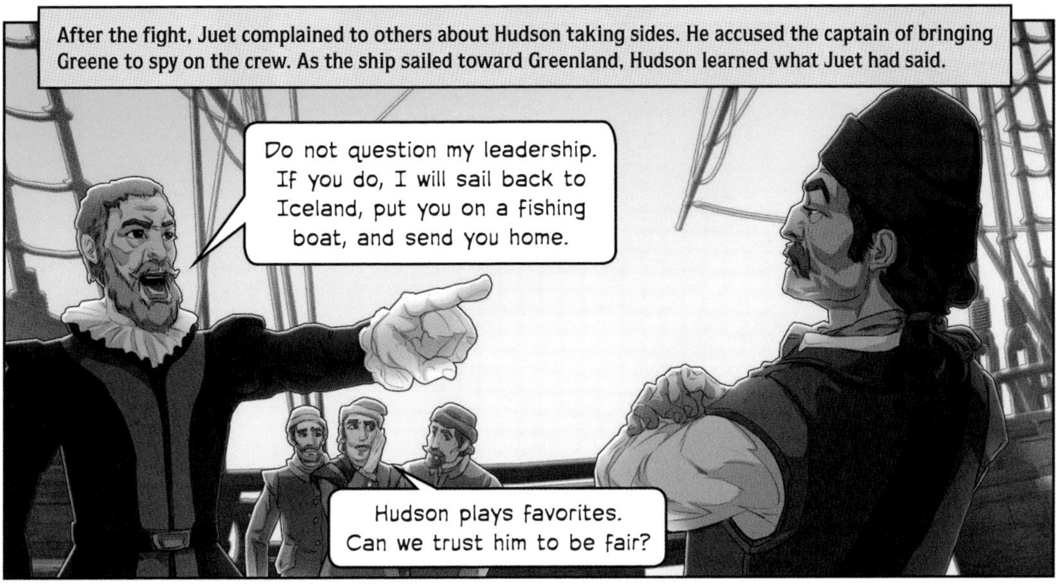
After the fight, Juet complained to others about Hudson taking sides. He accused the captain of bringing Greene to spy on the crew. As the ship sailed toward Greenland, Hudson learned what Juet had said.
Do not question my leadership. If you do, I will sail back to Iceland, put you on a fishing boat, and send you home.
Hudson plays favorites. Can we trust him to be fair?

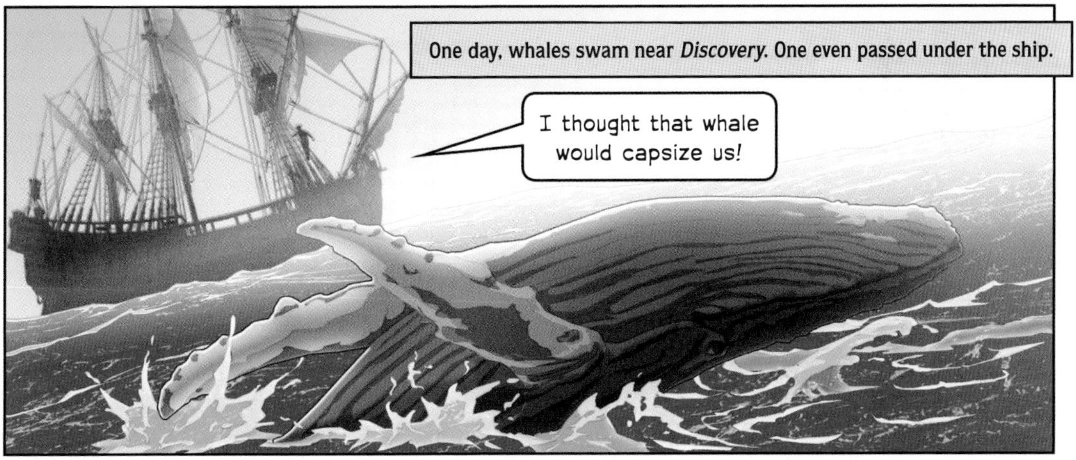
One day, whales swam near *Discovery*. One even passed under the ship.
I thought that whale would capsize us!

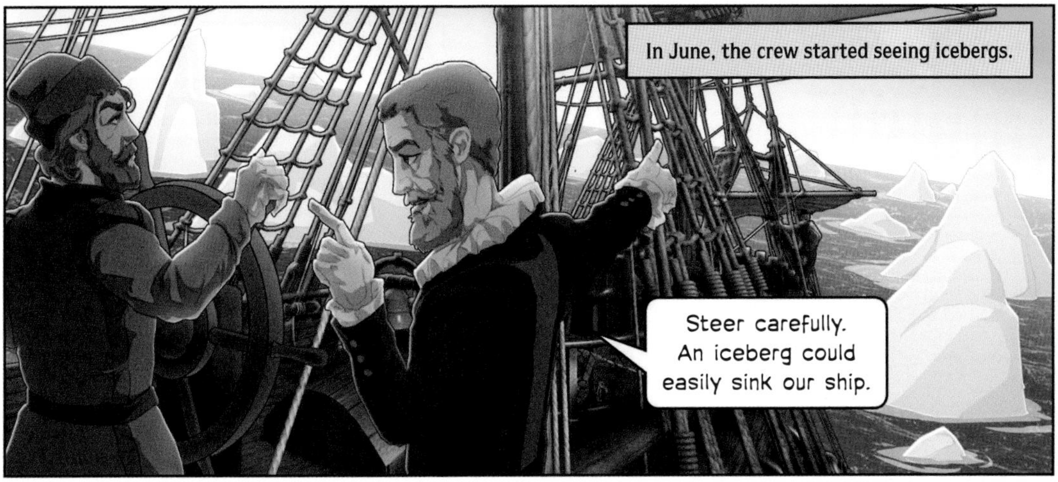
In June, the crew started seeing icebergs.
Steer carefully. An iceberg could easily sink our ship.

After passing Greenland, Hudson tried to sail northwest into Davis Strait. The strong current kept *Discovery* from going farther. So, Hudson sailed west instead. He ended up in what's now called Hudson Strait.

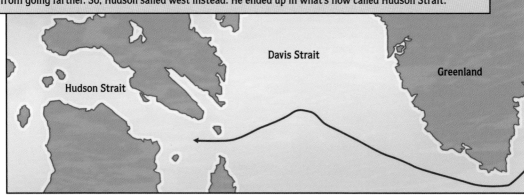

Davis Strait

Greenland

Hudson Strait

SPLOOSH!

Although it was summer, parts of the strait were full of ice. Some days, *Discovery* could barely move because of it. One day, a large piece of ice rolled over near the ship.

Some crew members began to worry. They feared they might die in icy waters far from home. In early July, Hudson gave the crew a choice.

Should we turn back or explore further for the Northwest Passage?

The crew voted.

If I had any money, I would pay it all to go home.

We have come this far. I say we keep going.

It is decided. We will continue our search.

The weather grew warmer. Some of the sea ice melted. *Discovery* was able to sail through Hudson Strait. In early August, the ship reached a vast area of open water.

This looks like a sea to the west. Does Asia lie on the other side?

After nearly four months of sailing, Hudson believed he might have reached the Northwest Passage.

Pricket and others took a shallop to explore an island. They found edible plants and many birds.

We should stay awhile to hunt and gather plants. We could use them for food later.

No. Our goal is to reach Asia. We must press forward.

Discovery set sail, but not in the direction the crew expected. Hudson set a course south instead of west.

For the next month, *Discovery* sailed south. The crew began to lose patience. On September 10, Juet openly mocked Hudson's route.

We aren't near Asia. We are wandering in the middle of nowhere!

Do not question your captain's plans.

Hudson fired Juet as mate. He also fired Francis Clements. He chose others to take their positions.

Over time, it became clear *Discovery* had not reached an ocean. It was in a large bay. Today, this body of water is called Hudson Bay.

We are making no progress. I have no faith in our captain's judgment.

In late September, *Discovery* sailed into what's now called James Bay. It lies at the southern end of Hudson Bay. It seemed the crew had reached a dead end.

A dense fog soon settled over James Bay. The crew could not see rocks or other dangers, so they stopped sailing. *Discovery* was stranded for a week. But Hudson was eager to get moving again.

Raise anchor!

It's too dangerous to sail in this fog.

We need to push on before cold weather comes. If we don't, the water will freeze. We will be stuck.

AGH!

The captain acted against our advice. Now look what's happened!

Discovery set sail, even though the waters were rough. Soon after, a large swell of water rocked the boat. Several men were injured. The ship also lost its anchor.

Discovery continued to face challenges. At the southern tip of James Bay, the ship became stranded on the rocks for half a day.

By the mercy of God, we are unharmed.

More and more, the men questioned Hudson's judgment.

Again the captain led us into danger.

I'm afraid we won't make it home alive.

Yet *Discovery* continued exploring James Bay. The crew grumbled.

We keep sailing around the bay. What is the purpose?

As November began, the crew grew even more restless. They had been at sea more than six months. They had hoped to be in Asia by now.

The weather grew colder.

Soon the whole bay will freeze over. The ship might get crushed by ice if it stays in the water. We must take it ashore.

The crew searched along the southeastern shore of James Bay. Finally, they found a spot that wasn't too rocky. They safely anchored *Discovery*.

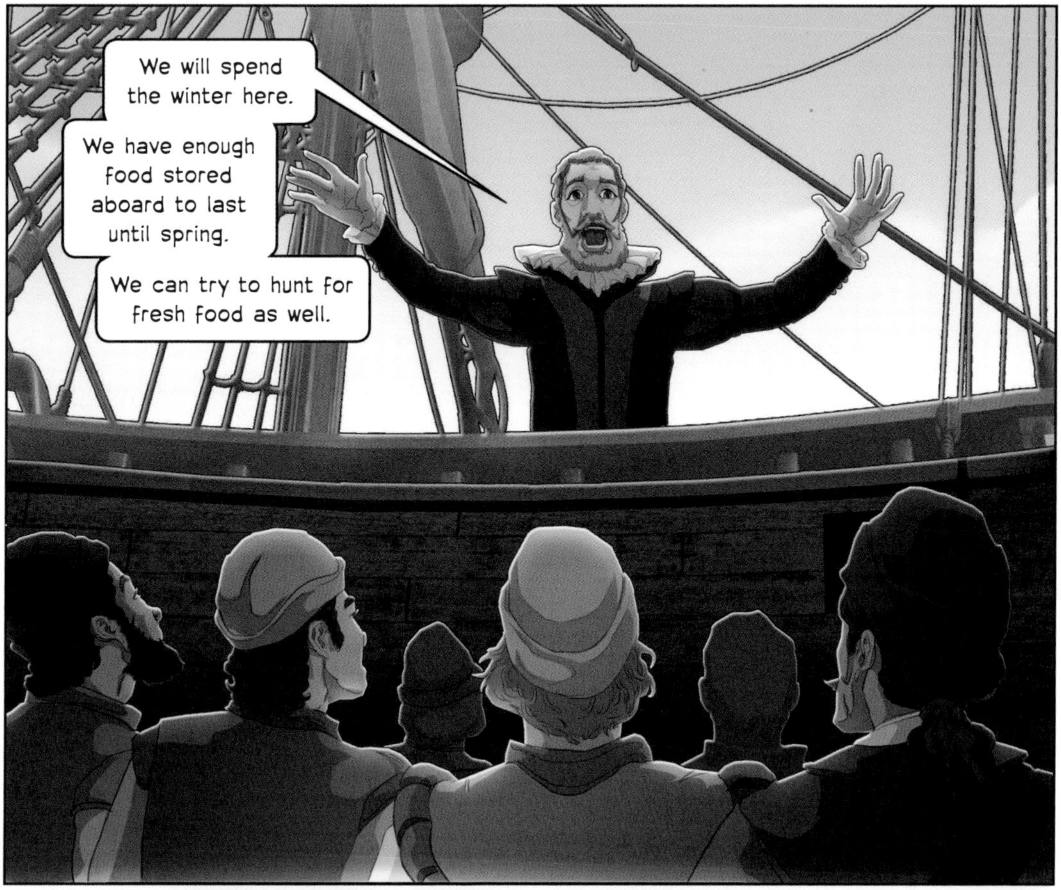
We will spend the winter here.
We have enough food stored aboard to last until spring.
We can try to hunt for fresh food as well.

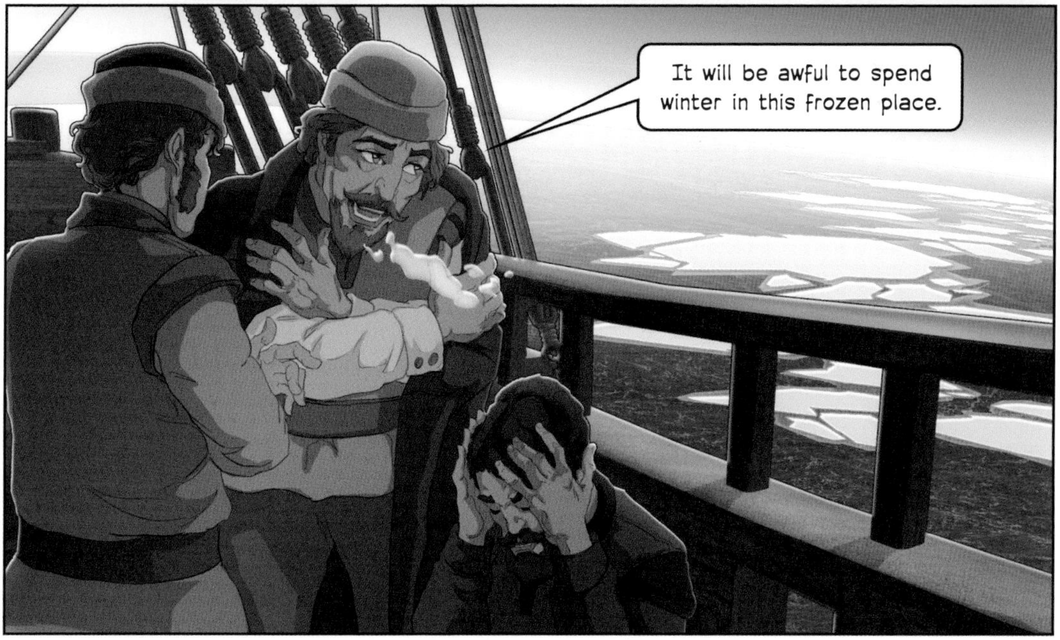
It will be awful to spend winter in this frozen place.

The harsh conditions proved dangerous. In mid-November, crew member John Williams died after spending too long outside in the cold.

When someone died at sea, his belongings were usually sold to other crew members. But Hudson gave the dead man's coat to his friend Greene.

More disagreements soon followed. Hudson told Philip Staffe, the ship's carpenter, to build a shelter on shore. Staffe refused.

The next day, Staffe went ashore to hunt. Greene joined him. This angered Hudson.

I am taking back the coat.

You can't. You already gave it to me.

I am in charge. I will do what I please.

Soon, several crew members had pitched in to build the shelter. Still, Hudson's actions toward Staffe and Greene left hard feelings.

As the crew settled in, tensions seemed to ease. The men focused on daily tasks. They cut wood for fires and hunted birds. They gathered plenty of fresh food.

England is never like this!

The long winter months passed slowly. Some of the crew lived in the shelter. Others stayed on *Discovery*. All suffered from the extreme cold. It sometimes got so cold that icicles formed on the men's beards.

Thank you! This really helps.

Fresh food became harder to find. The crew ate from the food stored on the ship. Still, many men grew weak and ill. The ship's doctor made a tea from tree buds to treat illness.

By May, the ice in the bay began to melt. Soon after, an Indigenous trapper visited. Hudson traded a knife, a looking glass, and buttons for two beaver skins. He also traded a hatchet for two deer skins.

As the ice kept melting, the crew went fishing in the shallop. One day, they caught 500 fish.

This gives me hope we will have enough to eat for a while.

Hudson took the shallop to search for more Indigenous people to trade with. He returned a week later. He had found no one.

The captain should have been focused on preparing to leave, not on trading.

In mid-June 1611, the crew brought *Discovery* back into the water. They had been stranded for more than six months. They had been cold and often hungry. But all were still alive except for Williams.

The men were eager to sail for home.

I am sorry. This is all the bread that remains.

I think there is more. Hudson must have hidden some away for himself and his favorite crew members.

Before they left, Hudson had handed out rations from the food on board. He had given each man a pound of bread. He had also sent some of the crew fishing. But they had caught very little.

The bread was supposed to have lasted the men two weeks. Most had finished their ration in a few days. So Hudson had given out cheese. Some of it was moldy.

I still think Hudson is hiding the best food.

I gave some good and bad cheese to each man. That makes it fair.

With food running low, the ship started out of James Bay. The crew expected to sail north and then east toward England. Instead, Hudson ordered the ship to sail west. He still wanted to search for the Northwest Passage. Crew members were unhappy.

We've done enough exploring! We have been gone more than a year already.

Even in June, ice remained in the bay. Days after leaving, *Discovery* got stuck in frozen waters.

Our troubles keep getting worse!

This is just another example of what a poor captain Hudson is.

Our food is almost gone.

How will we survive?

The men grew hungrier. Hudson ordered a search for any bread that crew members might have hidden away. They found 30 loaves. Had the loaves been stolen? Were they rations being saved for later? It wasn't clear. Still, Hudson took the bread and divided it among the men.

Mutiny!

By June 21, several crew members had grown ill. Others feared they would soon starve. They became desperate.

Hudson will not give up his search for the Northwest Passage.

There is only one way to save ourselves. We must take over the ship.

That evening, Henry Greene and William Wilson told Pricket their plan. They would force Hudson and those who supported him into the shallop. Then they would set them adrift.

Once we are rid of Hudson, we will sail for home.

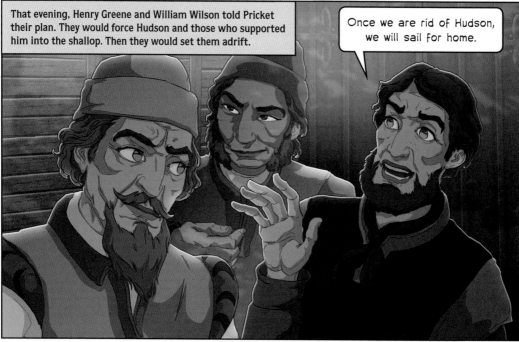

You can't do this! England hangs people for mutiny.

If we don't, we won't make it back to England at all. We will starve abroad.

Greene and Wilson left. Then Juet came to Pricket. He reported that other men were ready to join the mutiny.

Let me talk to Hudson. Maybe I can reason with him.

The time for talking is past.

Please, wait. Do not do this foul deed in the middle of the night like thieves.

The men agreed. They would wait, but only until morning.

When Hudson came out of his cabin the next morning, several crew members grabbed him.

Some men were still loyal to their captain. John King tried to fight, but the rebels overpowered him.

Hudson, his son, and seven supporters were forced into the shallop.

SCHNK!

The shallop was cut loose, and *Discovery* sailed away. Henry Hudson and the others were never seen again.

Discovery began the long voyage home. The rebels searched the ship for food. They found some biscuits, butter, peas, and pork in the hold.

I knew Hudson was hiding food.

We were right to take over the ship.

In late July, the crew stopped on an island to hunt. They met local Inuit and were attacked while trading. Pricket was injured. He survived. But four other men, including Greene and Wilson, did not.

Now there are only nine of us left to run the ship.

Discovery sailed on. The stores of food soon ran out. The men ate birds they had hunted. Then they gnawed the bones.

In late August, Juet died of hunger. All those who had led the mutiny were dead.

In October 1611, *Discovery* finally reached London. Only 8 of the 24 original crew made it back.

Authorities asked about Hudson. The survivors told what had happened. They said they had been starving. They blamed the mutiny on men who had died on the journey home.

Let's put this all behind us.

Nearly seven years later, Abacuk Pricket and three other men from *Discovery* stood trial for Hudson's death. None were found guilty.

Note: Most information on Hudson's final voyage comes from Pricket's journal. Pricket knew he would go on trial for Hudson's death. So how trustworthy is his account? Did Pricket make Hudson look bad to help his case? Did he change his journal after the mutiny? We will never know.

After Hudson disappeared, the *Discovery* and other English ships returned to the area he had explored. The crews still searched for the Northwest Passage. They found no signs of the shallop. More than four centuries later, Hudson's and the other men's fates remain a mystery.

MAP OF THE EXPEDITION

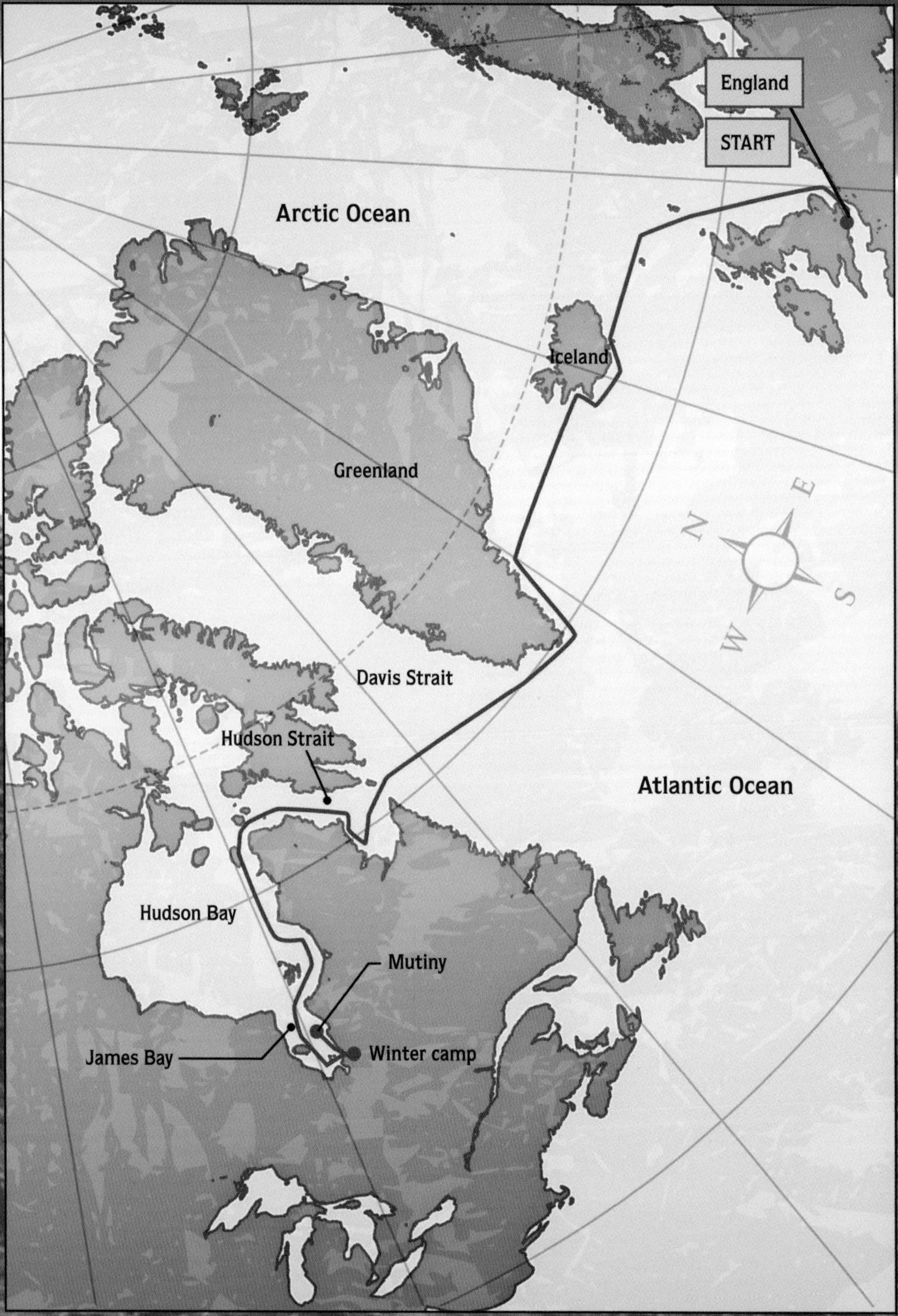
England
START
Arctic Ocean
Iceland
Greenland
N
E
S
W
Davis Strait
Hudson Strait
Atlantic Ocean
Hudson Bay
Mutiny
James Bay
Winter camp

MORE ABOUT HENRY HUDSON

At first, Henry Hudson may seem like a failure. He made four voyages trying to find a northern passage—a direct water route from Europe to Asia. He failed each time. On his fourth voyage, his crew mutinied. No one knows exactly what happened to Hudson. He and his followers may have died while adrift in the bay. They may have reached land and later starved.

The search for the Northwest Passage continued. No one found it until 1906. But the passage was icy. It was too dangerous to be used as a trade route to Asia. In the meantime, other safer and easier routes had been found.

Over time, historians began to appreciate the things Hudson did accomplish. Hudson had explored the harbor beside what is now New York City. He had explored what is now called the Hudson River. The bay where he likely died also bears his name.

Hudson's journeys set the stage for later voyages. Other people further explored the east coast of what is now the United States. They sailed to what is now northern Canada. Today, historians credit Henry Hudson as being a skilled navigator and explorer. His deeds, like the mystery surrounding his death, live on.

GLOSSARY

bay (BAY)—a body of water set off from an ocean or other larger mass of water, partly closed in by land

capsize (KAP-sahyz)—to overturn in the water

hold (HOLD)—the place under the deck of a ship where things are stored

Indigenous (in-DIJ-uh-nuhss)—a way to describe the first people who lived in a certain area

Inuit (IN-yoo-it)—a native person, or a group of native people, from the Arctic region north of Canada, Alaska, Greenland, and Russia

investor (in-VEST-or)—a person who puts money into a project or idea hoping to make more money in the end

mate (MEYT)—an officer on a ship

mutiny (MYOO-tuh-nee)—the act of trying to take away control from a person in charge, especially among sailors

navigator (NAV-ih-gay-tor)—the person who sets the course of a ship or aircraft

ration (RASH-un)—a set amount of something given to a person, often in times of shortage

shallop (SHAL-up)—a small boat with oars or sails, used mostly for short trips in shallow water

strait (STREYT)—a narrow waterway connecting two larger bodies of water

voyage (VOY-ij)—a long trip, often by water and often to a faraway place

READ MORE

Faust, Daniel R. *The Real Story Behind the Age of Exploration.* New York: PowerKids Press, 2020.

Hazleton, Amie. *Henry Hudson: An Explorer of the Northwest Passage.* North Mankato, MN: Capstone, 2017.

Hyde, Natalie. *Search for the Northwest Passage.* New York: Crabtree Publishing, 2017.

INTERNET SITES

DK FindOut: Explorers
dkfindout.com/us/history/explorers/

Ducksters: Henry Hudson
ducksters.com/biography/explorers/henry_hudson.php

PBS World Explorers: Henry Hudson
pbslearningmedia.org/resource/pbs-world-explorers-henry-hudson/pbs-world-explorers-henry-hudson/

AUTHOR BIO

John Micklos, Jr. has written more than 60 children's books spanning a wide range of ages and genres. His work includes picture books, poetry books, and numerous nonfiction books. He enjoys visiting schools and conducting writing workshops with students.

ILLUSTRATOR BIO

Martín Bustamante is an illustrator and painter from Argentina. At the age of 3, he was able to draw a horse "starting by the tail," as his mother always says. As a teenager, he found inspiration in movies like *Star Wars* and comics like *Prince Valiant*, which were full of fascinating worlds of colors, shapes, and atmospheres. At that moment, drawing and painting became his passions. He started working as a professional illustrator and has worked for several editorials and magazines from Argentina, the US, and Europe.